JALAPEÑO KILLER

A Mexican Café Cozy Mystery

HOLLY PLUM

Copyright © 2017 by Holly Plum

All rights reserved. No part of this publication may be reproduced, stored in or introduced into a retrieval system, or transmitted, in any form, or by any means (electronic, mechanical, photocopying, recording, or otherwise) without the prior written permission of the copyright owner of this book.

This is a work of fiction. Names, characters, places, brands, media, and incidents are either the product of the author's imagination or are used fictitiously. Any resemblance to actual persons, living or dead, business establishments, events, or locales is entirely coincidental.

CHAPTER ONE

"Don't say another word." Mari Ramirez clenched her jaw as she tried to think of reasons why she'd thought a family beach vacation was a good idea.

For the past three hours, she'd been trapped in the middle seat of a van with her two little brothers, Alex and David, on either side of her. Although they were both twenty-something years old, they fought like children. Mari's mother, who had taken the passenger's seat, had insisted on Mari sitting between them to keep them from arguing. It hadn't worked.

"David posted online that we're going to Pelican Point," Alex said. "I didn't tell Nina I was leaving town, and now she wants to know why she wasn't invited. Thanks a lot, David."

"Aren't you supposed to bring your girlfriend on vacation?" David argued. "I don't see why it's a big deal."

"I've been with her three weeks, and she's already way too clingy," Alex responded. "Plus, she keeps asking about you."

"I can't say I don't blame her." David smirked.

"What? Bro, you didn't." Alex held up a fist and Mari instinctively pushed it away.

They had been arguing like this, back and forth, from the moment they'd left their tiny Texas hometown. At around lunchtime, David had insisted on stopping to eat while Alex had demanded that they drive straight to Pelican Point.

Mr. Ramirez had settled for stopping at a gas station, but Alex and David had fought over who got to use the restroom first.

They drove on for the next hour, David and Alex making wordless gestures at each other behind Mari's back while she stroked her bulldog, Tabasco. Behind them in the back seat, her Abuela named Josefina napped restlessly. It was the hottest part of the afternoon. Sweat soaked through the t-shirt Mari was wearing, and no one seemed particularly happy to be headed to the Gulf Coast.

Mr. Ramirez had only agreed to an extended vacation after much pestering from his wife, who felt he had been spending too much time at the family restaurant. Mrs. Ramirez was elated to be finally embarking on the week-long holiday for which she had been looking forward to for months. Mr. Ramirez, however, seemed aloof and preoccupied. Every few minutes his phone lit up with a new text, and he struggled to respond with one hand.

"You shouldn't text and drive," Mari said bluntly. "You're not very good at it."

"What's the worst that could happen?" Mr. Ramirez asked, once again taking his eyes off of the road.

"I think parents should be forced to take technology classes," David muttered. "I'm looking at you, padre."

"You're one to talk," Alex began but stopped as Mari's spray bottle that she used to discipline Tabasco came dangerously close to his face.

"We're almost to the beach, but we're not going to make it if we die on the way there," Mari stated, taking a deep breath. "Who are you texting, anyway?"

David shrugged. "Three guesses who."

"For your information," Mr. Ramirez replied from the driver's seat, "I'm texting your uncle, Diego."

Mari groaned. Her father had spent the past week painstakingly interviewing the staff at Lito Bueno's Mexican Restaurant to determine who among them was worthy to run the restaurant during his absence. Finally, at the last minute, he'd announced that he was bringing in outside help consisting of his little brother Diego and Diego's daughter Cammie. Diego owned a seafood restaurant of his own in College Station that was perpetually in danger of being shut down by the health department. Where Mr. Ramirez was cool and professional, Diego was clumsy and inept. Mari and her brothers could think of no reason why their father had left him in charge of the restaurant, other than that he was a Ramirez.

"How are they handling things?" Mari asked.

"Not well," Mr. Ramirez said grimly. "Diego accidentally filled the sugar jar with salt. He said it was Mateo, the bus boy, but I know it was him. Apparently, customers have complained."

"He's only been there three hours," Mari responded. "I don't know why you didn't leave the restaurant to Chrissy. She has been working there the longest."

"I think we should go back," Mr. Ramirez stated anxiously. Mari suspected, from the tone in his voice, that he had been thinking this for the past hour. "At the rate, my brother is going, it's only a matter of days before he burns the place down."

"We're not going back," Mrs. Ramirez firmly replied. "It took you long enough to agree to make this trip, and I intend to enjoy myself."

"I won't be surprised if we lose half of our regular customers," Mr. Ramirez went on, as though she hadn't spoken. "Think of the money."

"Don't be silly. Our regulars know that we're out of town." Mrs. Ramirez placed a steady hand on her husband's arm. "Mari went through great pains to rent us a condo, and it was the best deal she could find. We will be throwing money away if we turn back."

The thought of losing more money seemed to have a sobering effect on Mr. Ramirez. He lapsed into a troubled silence. Mrs. Ramirez grinned proudly.

Mari glanced out the window at the plains on either side of them, dotted with water towers and oil derricks. The one great thing about driving through Texas was that even at its most monotonous, it was remarkably beautiful in its own way. As they approached the coast, the fields subsided and were replaced by storefronts and coastal views.

Mari's family had settled on Pelican Point because it was quieter, smaller, and cheaper than other southern beach towns. Mr. Ramirez had also put up a fuss about not wanting to spend money to visit a place with rowdy, drunk college students. Pelican Point was better than no vacation at all. Mari had found the nicest condo she could in the price range that her father was willing to spend. She'd crossed her fingers that they would have enough fun to want to go back again the following year. All of them needed a break from the family restaurant.

"We're here," Mr. Ramirez said, bringing the van to an abrupt halt. They had pulled up outside a white three-story building within view of the beach.

"The owner should be here any minute to give us the keys to the condo," Mari instructed.

Glancing down the street, Mari saw rows and rows of identical white buildings. The door of one opened and a woman in a red swimsuit descended the stairs with a towel draped around her waist. Alex let out a low whistle, and Mari elbowed him sharply.

The family got out of the van and into the cool shade of the lobby. The owner of the condo proved to be a smiling, affable woman in her mid-forties wearing a broad straw hat and a white pantsuit.

"My name is Shannon May," she said, shaking each of their hands in turn, "and I can't tell you how delighted I am that you've chosen to spend the week with us." She struck Mari as a classic Texan, all charm, and politeness.

"So far so good," Mari muttered to Tabasco.

"The great thing about Pelican Point," Shannon continued as she led them into the blinding sunlight, "is the size. Everything you'll need to make yourself at home during your visit lies within a few minutes' walk to the beach."

Mari had given this same sales pitch to her family when she'd convinced them to book a condo instead of a hotel room, but she nodded along as Shannon rattled off a long list of oceanfront shops and restaurants.

"Sounds great," she added politely.

"And you picked the perfect week to vacation here," Shannon responded. "This week we're hosting the annual Pelican Point Seafood Festival, which is probably my favorite event of the year. The smell of oysters and shrimp po'boys wafting down the street from all directions is heaven."

"I wouldn't dream of missing it," Mr. Ramirez said eagerly. "I'm hoping to meet some of the local fishermen while I'm here. Our family owns a restaurant near hill country, and we're always hunting for cheap seafood suppliers."

"Oh, hill country," Shannon replied, flashing two rows of perfect teeth. "My husband and I have been camping there. Have you folks ever been to Tortoise Nation?"

"Funny story," Alex chimed in. But Mari placed her hand over his mouth. She had no intention of telling a stranger about the deadly events that had taken place on their previous family vacation.

"Anyway, my husband fishes for a living." Shannon smiled. "I have to drag him away from work."

"What's his name?" Mr. Ramirez asked.

"Maurice." Shannon pointed to the sea, shielding her face with one hand. "Right now he's down at the docks about to set out on his boat. He loves that thing. I always say he should have married it."

Mrs. Ramirez chuckled sympathetically.

Shannon led the Ramirez family to their condo. Upon entering, Mari realized why she had managed to rent it for such a low price. Although it wasn't shabby, there was hardly enough room for the entire family to convene in one place. She began to wonder, with a sour feeling in her stomach, whether the entire week was going to be similar to her experience of being stuck in the car with them.

"I realize it's a bit crowded," Mari said as soon as Shannon left, "but it's nice." She waved in the direction of the living room wall, which was bare except for a calming painting of the ocean. "Abuela gets her own room. I'm sharing with Tabasco so I can keep him out of Dad's hair, and Alex and David get the couch."

"Wait, you mean we don't get a room of our own?" Alex responded, sounding annoyed

"There's a storage closet if you want it," Mrs. Ramirez added.

"Honestly, there's enough room on the couch bed, and you'll be steps away from the fridge." Mari took a deep breath, hoping that her brothers wouldn't mind. She knew they would be at the beach most of the time anyway.

Sensing that another fight was imminent, Mari followed her father and Abuela down the hallway and claimed a room. A couple of Van Gogh prints hung on the wall above a queen-size bed. A small nightstand stood to one side of the room, topped with a single vase of plastic flowers. In a drawer at the bottom of the stand, Mari found a couple of vintage paperbacks. One of them was an Agatha Christie novel.

She laughed. Mari didn't intend on getting wrapped up in any sort of mystery while she was on vacation.

Setting her suitcase down on the floor by the bed, Mari left the room in search of the bathroom. Finding it already occupied by her mother, she followed the trail of sunlight down the hall to a pair of sliding glass doors which led to a small outdoor patio. A white hammock hung from the railing, blown by a light breeze. A couple of wicker chairs sat facing the shore. Standing in the doorway, she heard the steady pulse of the surf and the lone cry of gulls far out at sea.

She was beginning to think that things would work out great when the peace was disturbed by a loud banging inside.

"David, no way!" Alex yelled. "I'm getting a hotel room!"

The door to the bathroom flew open, and a red-faced Mrs. Ramirez came striding out with her hands on her hips. "Really?" she said. "You aren't going anywhere. This is the first real vacation we've taken as a family in a long time. I will not have you boys ruining it." She slammed the bathroom door.

The door of the bedroom across from Mari's opened and her father peered into the hallway. "Could y'all keep it down out there? I'm making a very important phone call."

This, however, proved to be the wrong thing to say.

"We've been here for *ten* minutes, José," Mrs. Ramirez shouted, leveling a gaze that could have destroyed the whole building. "Are you going to be on that darn phone this whole trip?"

"I have a restaurant to run," Mr. Ramirez responded, unflinching. "Diego changed the daily special again."

"Seriously?" David muttered. "Who cares what Uncle Diego does? We're at the beach."

"Quiet, Alex," Mr. Ramirez exclaimed.

"I didn't do anything," Alex replied. "Stop blaming me for David's mistakes. I hate it when you do that."

"I'm tired of all the disrespect." Mr. Ramirez rolled his eyes and slammed his bedroom door.

Mari's Abuela, who had just emerged from her bedroom wearing a modest black and white swimsuit and cover-up, stood with an expression of tranquil sadness. "It's just as loud here as it is back at the restaurant," she quietly commented in Spanish.

"Let's get out of here, Abuela," Mari said. "The beach is calling."

Josefina smiled and reached into her purse for her suntan lotion. Tabasco barked in response. Mari took a deep breath and escorted her Abuela outside.

CHAPTER TWO

Mari, Josefina, and Tabasco emerged from the condo into the warmth of a late summer afternoon. For a moment as the sun beat down on her back, Mari contemplated returning indoors and to read a novel in the cool of her room. But then, hearing her mother yelling again, she made up her mind.

"We'll have a good time even if no one else does," she said to her Abuela.

"Your Abuelo and I never fought like that," Josefina said sadly. "I warned your parents before they got married that they were going to have problems. They are both very stubborn."

"Don't I know it," Mari replied. "What about before they were married?"

"Ha!" Josefina chuckled to herself. "They were much worse. I think time has worn them down some."

Mari and Tabasco helped Abuela all the way across the street and to the entrance to the beach. After the irritating car ride and the chaos at the condo, the relative tranquility of the beach came as a blessed relief. Mari slipped off her sandals and buried her toes in the hot sand; her heart calmed by the murmur of the waves lapping against the shore. Far in the distance, she saw the outline of a fishing boat, half-obscured by the shimmering heat that was rising off the water.

The beach was nearly empty due to the blaring sun. Most of their fellow guests wouldn't emerge from their rooms until sundown. However, a few brave sunbathers had arranged chairs and towels for themselves some distance from the water and were either reading or soaking in the sun. Further down the shore, she saw the slim figure of the woman her brother had been ogling earlier, the one in the red bikini, lying with her back to the sun.

From what Mari had noticed on their drive, Pelican Point had only one main street called Pelican Street. The long stretch of road separated the condos from the beach. From her spot near the shore, Mari saw all the major shops and restaurants in town. On the back patio of a wood-framed seafood restaurant with brightly colored awnings, a man and a woman sat enjoying an early dinner. Further down the street stood a farmer's market with a large gazebo at its center.

Vendors lined the beach in the area surrounding the gazebo, their tables laden with crawfish, crabs, various fish, and fresh vegetables. But because the beach was so sparsely crowded, they had few customers and looked faintly bored. One woman had abandoned her station altogether and was pacing the sand in front of the gazebo. She had sandy-colored hair and was wearing a white shirt and hat, much like the outfit Shannon had been wearing. Mari figured they must all wear white here to keep cool during the hottest parts of the day.

It was all so serene; she half-wished she could retire here and spend her days wearing a knit top and a straw hat, walking Tabasco on the beach at sunset. She would never understand what kept her father tethered to their Mexican restaurant.

"I forgot my hat," Josefina said, reaching up and touching the top of her head. "Ay dios mio."

"I'll go back and get it," Mari replied. "Where did you leave it?"

"My bedroom."

Mari left Tabasco to watch over her and turned back in the direction of the condo. If she was quiet enough, she might be able to sneak in without being noticed by anyone. After being in the car with her family for nearly five hours, she felt a sudden yearning to rent a boat and go somewhere far out on the water where there wasn't a single person to bother her. Her Abuela could come too, of course. Josefina never bothered Mari.

As she was crossing the street, regretting that she had left her sandals on the beach, she heard barking coming from behind her. Turning back around, she saw a crowd of people converging on the center of the beach from all directions. At first,

Mari couldn't make out what it was. But as she began running back toward the beach, she realized everyone was standing around a body.

A wave of fear washed over her.

For a moment she couldn't think coherently. Mari felt like she was just a body, legs running as fast as they could go but still not fast enough. Denial welled up inside of her like a lump in the throat. The crowd parted to let her through, and the horrible truth was made plain.

Her Abuela was lying in the sand, and she wasn't moving.

CHAPTER THREE

The next few minutes felt like an eternity to Mari. She yelled at someone to call an ambulance. Then, brushing aside Tabasco who had been guarding Josefina against strangers, she knelt down beside her and felt for a pulse. To Mari's immense relief, Abuela was still breathing.

"Did anybody see what happened?" Mari asked.

The crowd of strangers stared back at her blankly. "We only just noticed she'd collapsed," said an older man. "We thought that maybe she had a heart attack."

Having solved crimes back home for quite some time, the possibility of a heart attack or some other natural ailment hadn't occurred to her. She wished Josefina would wake up so she could question her. She wished the ambulance would hurry up and get there.

Mari pulled her phone from her pocket as Tabasco circled Abuela. She dialed her father's number knowing that he was the only one paying full attention to his phone at the moment.

Mr. Ramirez picked up after three rings. "Marisol, I am trying to keep this like clear," he said, sounding distinctly irritated. "I'm waiting for another call from your uncle."

"Padre!" Mari shouted.

"I'll call you back in a minute." He hung up.

Mari slammed the phone down in the sand and let a growl of frustration that could have passed for one of Tabasco's. She spent the next few minutes shaking Josefina to coax her into waking up.

Determined to get hold of her family, Mari called both of her brothers. Neither one had answered, and she suspected this was because they were still arguing with each other. Her mother had turned off her phone on principle before they'd reached the condo, so her call went straight to voicemail.

"I hope she's okay," said one of the onlookers. A woman with silver hair and round sunglasses clasped her hands together as if in prayer. "It could be this heat, you know. My Earl worked in construction but had to retire last year after he suffered a stroke. They were building an offshore rig down near Corpus when he collapsed on the job. Even after that, he insisted on continuing to work, but the company encouraged him to retire early."

"At least I was given a generous retirement package, Darla" Earl chimed in, rubbing his bald scalp. "It's more than a lot of people get."

"Well, you worked there for thirty years," Darla replied to her husband. "It was the least they could do."

The couple continued to prattle on amiably. Mari drifted in and out of the conversation, grateful for their company even when she wasn't listening. It helped relieve some of the stress she was feeling.

After what felt like an hour, she heard the wail of sirens in the distance, and an ambulance turned off of Pelican Street onto the white sand. Two men in uniforms leaped out of the back carrying a stretcher, while a third questioned Mari about what had happened.

"I haven't been able to get her to wake up," Mari said, sounding more frantic than she intended. "Should I be worried?"

"She's waking up now," Darla commented. And indeed Josefina began to stir, opening her eyes groggily and looking around. Tabasco barked happily.

"Where am I?" she asked. "What happened?"

Mari knelt down beside her. "Abuela, you passed out. These men are going to take you to the hospital to make sure you don't have any head trauma. You'll be fine." She felt reassured that her words would hold true.

Josefina nodded weakly. "There was a man. Did you see him?"

"Yes, these men will take you to the hospital," Mari replied. "I'm still trying to get hold of the rest of the family. When I do, I'll come and see you."

As Josefina was loaded onto the stretcher, she reached for Mari with a look of infinite sadness. "I'm so sorry for ruining your vacation," she said.

Mari squeezed her hand firmly. But before she could respond, the paramedics pushed the stretcher with a loud clatter into the back of the ambulance. Josefina waved weakly as the doors closed.

The ambulance rattled back up the sandy path and onto Pelican Street.

As it disappeared into the distance, Mari took out her phone and called her dad again.

"Hello." His voice was just barely audible over the sounds of yelling in the background and what sounded like a shoe being beaten against a counter. "What is it this time?"

"There has been an accident. Abuela has been taken to the hospital. I'm about to head over there, and I thought it would be nice—"

"Just a second." Mr. Ramirez cleared his throat. "Will you keep it down in there?" In a quieter voice, he added, "Where are you?"

"I'm still on the beach," Mari replied.

"We'll be right over." He hung up again.

Mari returned her phone to her pocket, wondering if agreeing to come along on vacation had been a bad idea. Trouble seemed to follow her wherever she went. Already she saw her brothers running across the street toward her. She wondered if they would all blame her for Abuela's injury.

"Hi," she said when they were close enough to talk, "where's Mo—"

But at that moment there came a tremendous noise from behind her like a hundred guns firing.

Instinctively, Mari flung herself down onto the sand. She heard screams as the remaining sunbathers ran across the beach. Alex and David covered their ears and glanced toward the water squinting.

"Look at that," Alex shouted, pointing to the shoreline.

Mari sat up, shocked by what she saw. Smoke billowed over the water. Beneath it, a fishing boat had been consumed in flames. Mari's eyes went wide.

"I don't believe it," Earl gasped. He stood quietly next to his wife, Darla. "That looks like Maurice May's fishing boat. I hope he's okay."

"I don't think so, dear," Darla replied.

***

Mari didn't know what became of Maurice May and she didn't have time to stay and find out. David and Alex led her to the van where her parents were quietly waiting. They looked supremely irritated and didn't appear to be speaking to each other.

"Mari, do you want to leave Tabasco at the condo?" her dad asked. It didn't sound like a suggestion.

"There's no time," Mari replied. "If they want to give me grief about it at the hospital, then they've picked the wrong day to mess with me."

Ten minutes later they arrived at the hospital, a shabby two-story unit with pirate emblems hanging from the walls and large plastic palm trees decorating the lobby.

"That dog is just adorable," said the nurse, a redheaded young woman with furiously red freckles. "Is he a pug?"

"Bulldog actually," Mari responded. "Pugs look a bit different."

"Oh, of course," the nurse exclaimed. "I get the two mixed up sometimes."

"Is my mother-in-law going to be okay?" Mrs. Ramirez asked in a tone of mild frustration.

"You will have to wait and speak to her doctor," the nurse responded. "I'm just here to check on the machines."

"This is perfect," Mr. Ramirez muttered angrily. "I told you we shouldn't have brought Abuela."

"So, you would just have her sit alone at home while we play at the beach?" Mrs. Ramirez argued. "Your own mother? Well, why don't you just move her into a retirement home while you're at it?"

"At least she could have kept an eye on the restaurant," Mr. Ramirez added. "She knows how to whip Diego into shape."

"Here we go." Mrs. Ramirez rolled her eyes. "I swear if I hear another word about the restaurant—"

"If you're looking for someone to blame then blame me," Mari interrupted. "I'm the one who brought us here." Tabasco barked in response. "I'm tired of all the arguing. Just point your fingers at me and be done with it."

"Well, you have to admit, you are cursed or something," Alex said quietly. "Everywhere you go, trouble follows."

"And you're never far behind, Alex." Mari raised her eyebrows.

Alex looked stunned by her statement.

"She's right," Mr. Ramirez continued. "This vacation was timed badly. Now my restaurant is in shambles, and my own mother might die of heat stroke. What was I thinking?"

"She's not going to die," Mrs. Ramirez interjected. On the other side of the room, the redheaded nurse looked more and more uncomfortable. "You are the biggest drama queen I've ever met. Last week when we ran out of beans, you said it was the worst disaster since World War II."

"Everything we sell has beans," Mr. Ramirez shouted. "It *was* a disaster. Name a worse one then if you're so smart."

"I can name several." Mrs. Ramirez raised her voice to match his.

"Alright, you two," Mari said, ushering them toward the door. "I'm not going to stand here all day and listen to this, not when Abuela is suffering. You can go into the hallway and resolve your differences like responsible adults. Don't come back in until you've grown up."

She closed the door with a loud sigh. A second later it opened again, and a doctor came shuffling in.

"Dr. Bryant," the man said, shaking Mari's hand. "It looks like your grandmother hit her head pretty badly when she fell. She has a mild concussion and may suffer from post-traumatic amnesia."

"Will she recognize us?" Mari asked, alarmed.

"Yes, it's nothing as serious as that," Doctor Bryant responded. "But she might not remember the events leading directly up to her accident. Her memory of this afternoon will be hazy, at best."

Mari frowned. How were they ever going to find out what had happened if Abuela couldn't remember?

"Dang, Abuela," David muttered.

"It could have been a lot worse," the doctor went on. "You're lucky you brought her in when you did. Staying in the heat at her age, given the level of humidity we had today, is not wise."

"Is she going to have to stay in our condo the entire trip?" Mari asked.

"Not necessarily, but you do need to be careful. Wear sunscreen at all times, and don't let her forget her hat." He nodded.

The doctor left the room, and Mari turned to face her brothers. "I don't know what we're going to do. If it gets to the point where she has to stay inside, I'm not going back out on the beach. I don't want to leave her."

"We'll stay with her," David replied, though Alex glowered as though not wishing to be included in this promise.

Josefina stirred and opened her eyes. Mari ran to the side of the bed and knelt down beside her.

"Are you okay? The doctor says you fell and hit your head."

"Que?" Abuela answered. "Who are you?"

Mari's eyes went wide. "Abuela, it's me. It's *Marisol*."

"I know that." Abuela chuckled, garnering grins from Alex and David. "I feel fine, Mari. Apart from a splitting headache."

"You had us scared there for a minute," Alex added.

"I just need some rest," Josefina said. "This bed isn't the most comfortable thing, but it will do for now."

"Do you have any idea what happened?" Mari took a deep breath hoping for some answers.

Abuela shook her head. "All I remember is sand, lots of shouting, and that dog of yours."

Tabasco barked happily.

"Do you remember why you fell?" Mari asked. "It's important."

She shook her head again. "I remember leaving the condo. Everything that happened after that is a blur."

"She's not going to remember, Mari," David responded. "You heard what the doctor said. Give it a rest."

Feeling immensely frustrated, Mari took Tabasco and went out into the hallway. There was no sign of her parents, which came as a relief. Her resentment toward the rest of the family for fighting and spoiling their family vacation was beginning to weigh on her.

Take a deep breath, Mari, she told herself. *You will figure out how to fix this. You always do.*

Mari spent the next several minutes pacing the hall with Tabasco at her side.

Most hospitals made her anxious, but she found this one, which was virtually empty and whose walls were painted a frothy sea-green, oddly cheering. A cardboard cutout of a pirate wearing a black sailor's hat and jovially holding up a pint glass leered at her from the end of the hall.

Mari was surprised when she heard footsteps approaching and a second later Shannon May rounded the corner. Shannon clutched a bouquet of wildflowers and waved at Mari as soon as she saw her.

"Hi, there," Shannon said, flashing a bright smile. "I hope your family is doing alright."

"Shannon, what are you doing here?" Mari asked, wondering if she had heard about the explosion. "Is your husband here as well?"

"My husband?" she replied with an air of concern. "I actually came to see your grandmother. I heard she passed out on the beach. I wanted to make sure y'all were okay."

"Oh," Mari replied. "She could be better."

"So, she is awake then?" Shannon asked. "Oh, thank heavens. I thought she might like some flowers to cheer up her room. How long are they going to keep her here?"

Mari realized she had forgotten to ask the doctor this. "I'm not sure. She has a head injury. Poor Abuela doesn't even remember what happened. I've tried asking, but her memory is shot."

"She's lucky to have such a devoted granddaughter," Shannon replied. "I am sure she will be back to normal in no time."

"I hope so, but you never know with these types of injuries." Mari shrugged. "How did you find out about the accident?"

"It doesn't take long for news to travel in Pelican Point," Shannon answered. "I was sitting at my desk when I saw a notification from my social media account that an old lady just had a heart attack on the beach. From the description,

I knew it had to be your grandmother. I also heard the sirens."

"We still don't know if it was a heart attack," Mari replied. "To be honest, we don't have any idea what happened. The doctor said she might have a mild form of amnesia. So, we might never know."

"Isn't that just the worst?" Shannon said with a flick of her hair. But before Mari could respond a police officer came striding around the corner.

"Mrs. May?" the officer said in a grave tone. "I need to speak with you for a second."

"I should go," Mari said, glancing down at Tabasco.

"No, please stay," Shannon responded, laying a firm hand on her arm. For the first time that afternoon she wasn't smiling. "What's this about?"

"It's your husband," said the officer. "He was just involved in a boat explosion off of Pelican Beach. He didn't make it, ma'am. I am sorry."

CHAPTER FOUR

After the police officer had left, Shannon fanned her face. Her breathing quickened, and her cheeks went rosy. Shannon desperately looked for somewhere to sit.

"I don't believe it," she whispered. "We were so close to having enough money to retire. If he had sold the boat like I'd been asking him to, we would have had enough. Why doesn't he ever listen? Why *didn't* he listen?"

"Well, at least he died doing something he loved," Mari said delicately. "You said that boat was his life."

"I don't understand why the police think his death is suspicious," Shannon went on. "Did you understand what that officer was saying? What did he mean by all that?"

"You're just in shock, Mrs. May." Mari did her best to comfort her. "The officer said that they're investigating the cause of the explosion that's all." Tabasco added to the conversation by barking.

"We have no enemies," Shannon continued. "The boat was up to code, and Maurice always took every precaution. Who would do something like this? I mean ..." Shannon's words were cut off by tears.

"I'm sorry," Mari said, unsure of what else to say to her. "Whatever happened, the police will get to the bottom of it."

"I just ..." Shannon sniffed. "I don't understand. There must be some mistake."

Mari heard another shuffling of footsteps in the corridor and a man wearing khaki pants, a Hawaiian shirt, and large aviators came striding toward them, whistling a jaunty tune. Mari narrowed her eyes, wondering why the man was staring at them as if he were a familiar face.

"Bernie Gumble, Lead Detective with the Pelican Point Police Department," he said, flashing his driver's license.

"That doesn't tell me anything but your birthdate," Mari commented. "It's a driver's license."

"Oh, whoopsy," Bernie replied, reaching into his shirt pocket and pulling out his badge. "There's the little guy that makes the ladies swoon." He chuckled, but Mari didn't respond. "I will be working your husband's case, Mrs. May. I assure you that I will find out who killed your husband."

"How do we know he was even murdered?" Shannon asked. "Perhaps, it was some hooligan from another town. But why would they have hurt my Maurice?"

"There could have been lots of reasons," Detective Gumble replied. "Besides, ma'am, you don't know what your husband got up to in your absence. For example, just a few days ago your husband contacted the station claiming that he'd been receiving death threats. I hope you understand that I must take this seriously."

Shannon let out another sob as the detective casually petted Tabasco.

"Did you take it seriously a few days ago?" Mari chimed in, not sure whether to be mad or wildly confused by the detective's care-free attitude. "Maybe none of this would have happened. Have you thought of that?"

Detective Gumble laughed lightly. "Oh, of course, we did."

"I can't believe he never told me this," Shannon said, sounding truly hurt. "Of all the things to keep hidden from me."

"Sometimes spouses keep secrets to protect their partners," Detective Gumble added cheerfully. "One summer after our house was broken into, I didn't tell my wife. I worked the case and caught the bandits myself. My wife went about her business and never stressed over a single thing. It worked out great."

Both Mari and Shannon stared at him disbelievingly.

"Are you still married?" Mari muttered.

"I'll need to speak to you back at the station, Mrs. May." The detective ignored

Mari's comment completely. "In private. After all, this is a murder investigation."

"Okay," Shannon agreed.

Shannon and Detective Gumble left the hallway, and Mari wondered whether or not the detective would be able to give Shannon the closure she needed about her husband. She felt an inkling of curiosity, but she did her best to push it aside. She was on vacation.

Mari found her parents and brothers sitting in the waiting room. Two of them had their arms folded, and Mrs. Ramirez faced the wall with her back to the other three, reading on her phone.

"I'm just saying," David said, "if your girlfriend is going to blow up at you over a status update, maybe you don't belong together in the first place."

"First of all it was *your* status update," Alex argued, "and second, you said we were cruising down Pelican Street with a pair of new honies."

"I meant *homies*," David commented. "You know I'm a bad speller."

"No, you didn't." Alex slapped his shoulder. "That word doesn't even make sense in the sentence you wrote."

"No one reads those things anyway." David rolled his eyes.

"Uh, yeah they do." Alex raised his voice.

Mr. Ramirez nervously ran his hands through his hair. "I bet that's what he's doing now. I'm going to come home and discover that he's completely changed the menu. This is a nightmare we're living in, isn't it? Curse you, Diego!"

"Dad, snap out of it," David said. "You're starting to lose your cool." Turning back to Alex, he added, "You said you wanted to break up with that chick a week ago. I just did you a favor, bro. Is this the thanks I get?"

"That's my business," Alex replied. "You are always getting in my business. I *hate* that we have the same taste in women."

"No, we don't," David argued.

Not knowing what to say to this, Alex pulled out his phone and proceeded to give David proof.

Watching them on their phones, Mari thought about how long she had wanted to go on vacation with the family and felt a keen sense of disappointment that this was what it had turned into. There was no knowing when they might all be able to travel together again, especially if her abuela's health got any worse.

"Listen up, everyone," Mari announced, waving her arms in the air. "I've been doing some thinking, and I think we need to lay some ground rules if we want to enjoy the rest of our trip."

The three Ramirez men looked at her anxiously. "What do you have in mind?" Mr. Ramirez asked.

"Just some small adjustments so we're not at each other's throats," Mari replied. "This happens every time we go somewhere, and I know we're all sick of it. I am taking charge."

"That's so weird," Alex muttered. "I was just sitting here hoping someone would stand up and volunteer to boss me around."

"You see, this is what I'm talking about." Mari pointed at her brother. "Madre, you are not allowed to cook for the remainder of the trip. It makes you extra cranky."

"Excuse me?" Mrs. Ramirez said, turning around sharply.

"The same goes for you, Padre," Mari went on. "The kitchen will only remind you of the restaurant. I will be cooking."

"Here it comes," Mr. Ramirez commented. "I suppose you want us to give our phones as well?"

"You do want to have a good time, don't you?" Mari held out her hand. "We can all survive one week without screens. We used to do it all the time when we were kids."

"And it sucked," David said quietly.

Tabasco barked at him.

"It did not," Mari pointed out. "You had a great childhood. Now, everyone, please turn off your phones."

"Mari, I know you mean well," her father began, "but—"

"Then don't do it for me," Mari pushed on. "Do it for Abuela. We don't know how many family vacations she has left. I know it's a hard thing to think about, but we have to face the music here. Something really bad could have happened today. We could have lost her." The room fell silent. "Abuela's last memories could have been of all of us arguing over something unimportant."

"Fine," Alex agreed. "I'm keeping my phone ... but I'll turn it off during the day."

"Me too," David said.

"Alright." Mrs. Ramirez put her phone in her pocket and looked at her husband.

"If the restaurant burns down, that's on you." Mr. Ramirez held his hands up in surrender.

"Finally and most importantly, I want y'all to promise not to complain, or shout, or argue while Abuela is in the room. She hates it, and she doesn't need the added stress." Mari nodded. "Does everybody promise?"

All four of them agreed.

"I won't cook," Mrs. Ramirez responded, "as long as you promise to make fish while we're here."

"You read my mind," Mari said, sensing that this was the best she could hope for. "Now let's enjoy our vacation."

"Can't wait," David responded with a wink. "I give Alex one hour before he breaks down and checks his messages."

"Ditto," Alex muttered.

"Oh, care to sweeten the pot?"

"You're on," Alex agreed.

CHAPTER FIVE

The next morning, Mari woke up early to find blue morning light slanting through her blinds. Josefina was sleeping peacefully in the next room. She had been discharged the night before. Doctor Bryant's examination had turned up no evidence of a heart attack or stroke, and the cause of her collapse on the beach remained a mystery.

After a quick shower, Mari put on her swimsuit and cover-up and rummaged through the refrigerator. It was empty except for a leftover pack of sports drinks from their journey. A box of sugary cereal that Alex had bought sat on the table. Craving breakfast tacos and remembering that Mrs. Ramirez had asked her to pick up fresh vegetables for that night's dinner, Mari leashed Tabasco and jogged down to the farmer's market. Luckily, it had just opened.

The morning sunlight gleamed golden on the empty beach, brightening the sand as she made her way through the stalls where groggy-eyed vendors were arranging their displays. Near the gazebo situated in the center, she spotted the sandy-haired woman she had seen the day before. The woman was clumsily attempting to put in her contacts before the first customers arrived.

"We'll pretend you didn't see that," she said conspiratorially as Mari approached the fresh produce booth. The wall behind her was lined with carrots, bell peppers, zucchini, cucumbers, onions, lettuce, mushrooms, oranges, and melons. "And I'd appreciate it if you didn't say anything to my boss about this. I suspect he would hate it if he knew I was getting ready at work."

"I don't know your boss," Mari replied. "But I do know a thing or two about working with difficult people." Tabasco barked in agreement.

The woman laughed. "Funnily enough, I don't know my boss either. I mean, I don't personally know the guy or gal who owns the farm where these veggies grow. I just sell the goods." She cleared her throat. "For all I know it could be *you*."

"I don't think we've been properly introduced," she said, extending her hand. "I'm Mari Ramirez. I am *not* your boss."

"Well then I'm Coco James," said the woman, shaking her hand limply. "Would you like a melon? I have more melons here than I know what to do with."

"I was looking for something more in the way of homemade salsa," Mari replied. "I'm frying up some fish tonight."

"Isn't that the greatest?" Coco commented as she led Mari back behind the counter among the rows and rows of tomatoes and bell peppers. "When I was a girl, my grandma and I used to make salsa every Memorial Day for my little league team. My grandparents owned a restaurant near Dallas. Here, smell this." She pulled the lid off a jar of Cajun spices, which Mari sniffed politely.

Coco proved remarkably chatty, and within ten minutes Mari had learned more about her than she knew about some of her friends back home. She learned that Coco had worked at a fancy corporate job in the city before deciding to simplify her life. "It's not the life my parents wanted for me," she said with a sigh, "but I guess I've always been drawn to the ocean. And food."

"Understandable," Mari replied. "It's beautiful here." She watched Coco bag up her items. "By the way, do you happen to know where I can find a good florist? The husband of the owner of the condo I'm renting died yesterday."

Coco's eyes widened with an expression of unmistakable surprise. "You mean Shannon May?" she asked.

"Yes, how did you know?"

"The entire town saw the boat explosion," Coco responded. "My friend Richard who sells oysters on the other side of the gazebo caught some of it on video. Of course, we all know Shannon, and the word around town is that she killed Maurice for the insurance money."

"She couldn't have done it, though," Mari pointed out. "She was in her office at the time. At least, that's what she said."

"Are you sure?" Coco responded, giving her a look of significance.

"She seemed awful upset yesterday." Mari nodded, remembering the shocked look on Shannon's face.

Coco shrugged. "We all do things we're not proud of. People can be cruel and mysterious. Anyway, that's just what I've been hearing."

"Yes, the town gossip," Mari said. Coco shrugged again and smiled. "I'm very familiar with that game, but I try not to play."

"Thank you for stopping by." Coco handed Mari her produce.

Mari and Tabasco strolled through the rest of the market before heading back toward home. Remembering that Shannon liked wildflowers, Mari picked up a bouquet at the florist that Coco recommended and called her on her way back to the condo.

"Hello, Shannon," Mari said, "are you in your office?"

Shannon sniffed loudly. "No, I'm taking the day off. I couldn't bring myself to go to work. I know it sounds crazy, but I haven't taken a day off in ten years. It feels strange, but it is the respectful thing to do I guess."

"There's nothing wrong with taking a personal day given the circumstances," Mari pointed out. "Anyway, I bought you some flowers because I thought it might cheer you up. Where are you?"

"I'm on the beach," Shannon answered. "I came out here to do yoga before dawn because I thought it might clear my head, but I ended up staying to watch the sunrise."

"I think I see you, actually," Mari said, waving as a slim figure in the distance turned to face her. "Be right there." She hung up.

A few minutes later she found Shannon sitting lotus-style on a lime green yoga mat. Her hair was tied up in a loose bun, and there were dark splotches on her face as if she'd recently been crying.

"I understand if you don't believe me," Shannon said as she took the bouquet in both arms, "but I swear Maurice never told me about those death threats he was getting. If he had, I would have gone straight to the police and demanded that they do something about it."

"Maybe Maurice was afraid that wouldn't solve anything," Mari commented. "The few encounters I've had with the Pelican Point Police Department have led me to wonder if they can really be trusted."

"Mari, they're going after the wrong person." Shannon flung the flowers down in the sand and broke into uncontrollable sobs. Tabasco sniffed the bouquet and couldn't resist tasting a flower. "Last night at the hospital, Detective Gumble told me that I am their number one suspect."

"Really?" Mari wasn't surprised to hear that the town gossip had turned out to be partly true. The police really did think that she was responsible for the boat explosion.

"The fact that they don't seem to know what they're doing isn't much comfort," she added. "I was planning on driving up north today and visiting my mother in Austin, but the police have asked me not to leave the area. Mari, it's only a matter of time before they arrest me."

"Not necessarily," Mari replied, not very convincingly. "They might find evidence suggesting that someone else committed the murder."

Shannon leaned forward and laid a well-manicured hand on Mari's arm. "Mari," she said, "I want you to think very carefully about what you saw yesterday. Can you remember anything about the boat explosion that could help me?"

Mari shook her head slowly. "I wasn't on the beach for more than a few minutes, and I was too focused on my Abuela. I was on my way back to the condo to retrieve her sun hat when I heard Tabasco barking. When I saw her in the sand, I thought she was dead. I was in a weird state of mind when the boat exploded. It all seems hazy now. Like a dream."

"I'm going to tell you something I haven't told anyone else, not even the police," Shannon whispered, drawing in a deep breath and speaking with great effort. "I think Maurice was having an affair."

The effect of this revelation was undercut somewhat by the fact that Mari's phone begun buzzing. "I'm so sorry," Mari said. "It's my mom."

"Mari, I need you to come home right away."

Mari was surprised to hear her father's voice. She wondered if he had somehow convinced his wife to lend him her phone to check in on the restaurant.

"Dad, you're not supposed to be—"

"It's important," Mr. Ramirez insisted. "Abuela is awake. She remembers what happened."

"I'll be right there." Hanging up the phone, Mari turned to Shannon and said,

"I think I've found someone who might be able to help you."

CHAPTER SIX

Mari walked into the condo to find Josefina seated at the kitchen table sipping water while the rest of the family sat around her. Mrs. Ramirez kept a hand on her mother-in-law as if she were made of porcelain. Alex and David continued to fan the room with a magazine so that Abuela would feel more comfortable.

"Yesterday I only remembered bits and pieces," Abuela said as Mari sat down beside her.

"What can you remember, Josefina?" Mrs. Ramirez asked.

"Should we call the police?" Alex said. "Of course, we'll need permission to use the phone." David smacked his brother, and Alex shook his head in apology.

"Pelican Point PD might not be able to do much," Mari commented.

"I trust Mari," Josefina said firmly. "She is just as capable as those police officers."

Mari smiled as she accepted her abuela's compliment. "How did you fall?"

Josefina nodded, but her eyes conveyed a profound sadness. "I'm not sure if I want to talk about it. Y'all will think I'm crazy."

"Don't be ridiculous," Mr. Ramirez replied.

"If it helps you feel any better," Mari chimed in, "I can send David and Alex out of the room."

"Hey," David and Alex exclaimed in unison.

"Alright," Josefina said with tranquility. "All I remember is a jalapeño. It was the jalapeño that did this to me."

Alex snickered in spite of himself and was summarily dismissed from the room.

"Do you remember anything else?" Mari asked after he had left. "What do you mean exactly when you say the *jalapeño* did it?"

Josefina shook her head and took another sip of her water. "It was that evil pepper. The jalapeño did this to me. I swear it."

"So, you're saying that a giant jalapeño emerged from the sea and attacked you," Mr. Ramirez clarified. "Oh, this trip just keeps getting better and better."

Josefina scowled. "That's what happened."

This time David snickered and removed himself from the room before he could be dismissed.

"If only we had something else to go on," Mari muttered, raking her hair with her fingers, "something that could help you make sense of what you remember. I don't question what you saw Abuela, but it would help if we knew more. Why would anyone attack you like that? You're not even a local."

Josefina excused herself to use the restroom, and Mari's parents turned to her with a worried look on their faces.

"A giant jalapeño?" Mrs. Ramirez whispered. "I don't like where this is going. We should consider leaving early."

"We could try and get her some police protection," Mari suggested. "If not from Pelican Point, then from somewhere nearby. I wouldn't want this *jalapeño* to come back."

"No one is after her," Mr. Ramirez said bluntly. "She has just gone loopy. It's brain trauma like the doctor said. There are no such things as giant peppers, and no one knocked her over at the beach."

"What if her mind is replacing a giant jalapeño with the actual man who hurt her?" Mari questioned him impatiently. "I know it doesn't make sense to us, but look at the bigger picture. She had a mysterious accident and minutes later; a boat exploded killing a man."

Mr. and Mrs. Ramirez frowned as if worried that the blow to Josefina's head had somehow affected Mari's brain, too.

"For now I think we ought to keep this story about the evil pepper between ourselves," Mr. Ramirez replied. "I think Abuela is confused and not remembering things correctly. I think we should keep her here the remainder of our stay."

"We could always—"

"No, Paula." Mr. Ramirez cut his wife off before she could finish her sentence. "We are not going home. I am not backing out on our rental agreement and losing hundreds of dollars."

***

That night Mari and her father fried some fresh grouper and made salsa from the tomatoes, onions, and jalapeño peppers she had bought at the farmer's market. With Mari's rules in place, and with everyone feeling relieved that Josefina was doing better, the family managed to get through dinner without any fights.

Once dinner was over, and the dishes had been cleared away, Mr. and Mrs. Ramirez pulled out a deck of cards and their sons joined them. Josefina, feeling much better than she had that morning, convinced her son to let her and Mari take one short stroll along the beach. The sun was going down, and a cool breeze swirled through the evening air.

"You really are okay, right Abuela?" Mari asked as she watched a couple of boys flying kites in the glow of the sunset. She glanced at the time. She'd promised her father that she would return to the condo promptly on the hour. She had about twenty more minutes.

"Your Padre thinks I'm loco," Josefina responded.

Mari wrinkled her nose. "You heard all of that?"

"I do have ears," she answered. "You kids think I'm made of chocolate flan or something. Jiggling all over the place."

"Just Dad." Mari sighed. "And don't take to heart anything he says. All he really cares about is the restaurant. Sometimes I wonder if he would survive a day if we sold it."

"He was always a hard-working little niño," Josefina added. "He just wants what's best for you and your brothers."

Mari stiffened her shoulders. She stopped on the sand and laid out a towel for them to sit. Mari watched the waves bearing down on the shore with Tabasco at her feet. It felt good to sit with the wind blowing through her hair, listening to the cry of gulls and the palm fronds rattling in the evening breeze. She half-wished she could stay there and not go back home, but she knew she couldn't do that.

Still, it would have been nice to visit the Gulf Coast more than once every ten years.

Mari's thoughts were interrupted by a piercing shriek from beside her.

"The jalapeño!" Josefina shouted, her face purple and splotchy, as she leaned into Mari. "It's that evil pepper!"

"What are you talking about? What's going on?" Mari's heart raced as she glanced around the beach. Tabasco barked like crazy.

"That thing that attacked me is here!" she cried.

Mari scanned the shoreline for any sign of a jalapeño pepper or anything close to it. All she saw was a little girl playing in the sand and few harmless sunbathers. "Abuela, take a breath. Tell me who you're looking at."

"The pepper," Josefina whispered, pointing at the sky. She shook Mari's arm, and Tabasco glanced up curiously.

"It's okay," Mari responded. "You are fine." She frowned, wondering if her father had been right all along. Her Abuela was making up things that weren't there. Was this brought on by her head injury or was it part of getting older? Or both?

"I think I'm ready to go back now," Josefina said after a long moment's silence.

"I think I am, too," Mari agreed, and together they rose and returned to the condo in the light of the dying sun.

CHAPTER SEVEN

Mari spent the next morning on the beach with her parents while her brothers stayed behind to be with Josefina. Tabasco barked in the wind and Mari did her best to keep him on his leash. She had yet to have anyone tell her that dogs weren't allowed in the sand.

"She's overwhelmed," Mr. Ramirez said. "Abuela needs some peace and quiet and then she'll be just fine." He sipped his coffee and turned his back to Tabasco as he took a bite of croissant.

"What do you think he's going to do, steal your breakfast?" Mari responded. She grabbed a croissant for herself. She'd walked to the local bakery only a few blocks away from their condo to buy them.

Mr. and Mrs. Ramirez ate their pastries and scanned through a free copy of the Pelican Point Press. Mari watched a couple of teen boys trying to surf, but their attempt at surfing had proven disappointing as the water was calm and untroubled.

"I wish we could have convinced Josefina to join us," Mrs. Ramirez said sadly. "It seems a waste to have brought her all this way only for her to end up in the hospital and hiding out in the condo."

"I tried to talk her into coming with us," Mari responded, taking another bite of her flaky croissant, "but she was afraid she would be putting the rest of us in danger if she went out. She's terrified of that jalapeño pepper."

Meanwhile, to the embarrassment of Mrs. Ramirez, Mr. Ramirez was flagging down locals and asking them where he could find the best deals on seafood. It didn't take him long to meet Earl and Darla, who visited Pelican Point once a year and raved enthusiastically about every restaurant in town except *Salt of the Sea*. Apparently, the wait staff wasn't very friendly.

"Dad, if you want to know where the best deals are you should ask the folks at the farmer's market up the road," Mari suggested. "When I go back to the condo I'm going to ask Josefina if she wants to go there with me. You're welcome to come if you want."

"Thanks," Mr. Ramirez replied, "but I've planted myself here, and this is where I intend to stay until I get hungry or another boat explodes."

"Suit yourself." Mari shrugged, though she felt relieved that he seemed to have finally discovered the concept of relaxation.

Getting Josefina out of the house proved surprisingly easy. She didn't like listening to her grandsons bicker, and she was perfectly willing to accompany Mari to the farmer's market.

"There are plenty of people around," Mari assured her as they wandered across tracks of loose sand, past an antique store with a *no shoplifting* sign prominently displayed in the window, and toward the farmer's market. "You have nothing to fear."

"Your father tried to tell me the same thing," Josefina commented.

Mari gripped her hand tightly as they approached the produce booth, where Coco was scrambling to pin up her hair before the first customers arrived.

"Running behind again?" Mari asked. "It's almost lunch time."

"My apologies," Coco said fervently. "My cat, Pearl, switched off my alarm clock again."

Mari felt sure that there was more to the story, but before she could inquire further, Abuela let out an ear-splitting shriek.

"Abuela," Mari gasped, startled. "What's wrong?"

Josefina raised a trembling hand to the wooden sign hanging above the produce stand. It read, "Produce from the Pros." Beside it, someone had painted a green jalapeño pepper.

"Is something wrong?" Coco asked, placing a hand on her chest.

"Everything is fine," Mari said to Coco. "Excuse us for a minute." Leading Josefina away from the stand and into the cool shade of the gazebo, she said, "Just relax, Abuela. It is only a drawing."

"It's a bad omen," Josefina replied, quietly pressing her palm to her mouth. "We shouldn't be here."

"I understand that you're worried," Mari began, "but I think you will find that there are jalapeño peppers just about everywhere that sells produce. You are bound to see them and pictures of them if you go looking."

"I understand that," Josefina responded with a hint of impatience in her voice. This is different, Marisol. I want to go home now."

"Alright." Mari sighed. "Wait here while I finish shopping and then we'll head back to the condo."

Mari left her Abuela sitting under the gazebo with Tabasco by her side and returned to the produce stand, where she found Coco applying eyeliner. Coco quickly dropped her makeup bag.

"How can I help you?" Coco grinned, her makeup half-finished.

"Sorry about that," Mari said as she examined a tomato that was overly ripe. "Abuela has been having some troubles the past couple of days, and I think your sign spooked her."

"Isn't it lovely?" Coco said, gazing up at it proudly. "That's Sean Herbert's logo. Everyone around here calls him Sean Pepper. He supplies us with …. well, peppers, of course."

"Sean Pepper," Mari repeated. "That's clever."

"Yeah," Coco continued. "People have been calling him that even before he got into farming. It's the tattoo on his arm of a giant, green pepper. A jalapeño if I'm not mistaken."

"Interesting," Mari replied. "And unique." She narrowed her eyes, wondering if this man had been to the beach recently.

Tabasco began to growl and bark persistently, so Mari finished paying for her produce and left the stand to find Josefina. But she hadn't gone more than a few paces before she heard a tremendous bang that sent chills down her spine. With an abruptness that was sickening to watch, the roof of the gazebo collapsed in on itself.

As people began running out of their booths, Mari fought her way through the newly gathered crowd hoping to find her Abuela intact. Horrible visions of her body buried beneath a pile of rubble filled her head.

"Abuela!" Mari shouted in desperation. "Abuela, can you hear me?"

Tabasco gave a final loud bark, and Mari turned around to find Josefina standing a few feet behind her. Gasping, Mari dropped her bag and ran forward to hug her.

"I came running as fast as I could," Mari said. "I honestly thought you were dead."

"Tabasco saw a bird and went running after it," Josefina explained. "I followed him and, well, you saw what happened."

"Abuela, your hands are shaking," Mari pointed out. "You look terrified."

"I don't want to talk about it," she snapped. "I told you I wasn't crazy and no one believed me."

"I believe you," Mari said.

"I know," Josefina responded. "I'm sorry. I'm just frustrated that no one else seems to be listening to me. It seems like once you've reached a certain age, no one takes you seriously anymore."

"They're going to listen now," Mari responded with surety, trying to make a connection between Abuela's accident and the man they called Sean Pepper. "Starting with the police."

There *had* to be a connection between the two.

CHAPTER EIGHT

Half an hour later Mari stood in the lobby of the Pelican Point police station with Josefina and her dog Tabasco at her side. On the way there, Mari had assured her Abuela that their concerns would be taken seriously. But her own words didn't inspire her with confidence. Upon entering the police station, a life-size poster of a pirate had been hanging on the wall much like the ones at the hospital.

"Is it pirate month or something?" Mari muttered, forcing out a smile.

A receptionist was seated behind the front desk with a flower lei draped around her neck. She was drinking what looked like a margarita from an enormous glass and listening to a local country station on low volume.

"Is Detective Gumble here?" Mari asked. "I met with him a couple of days ago and wanted to follow up on our last conversation."

"Sure, let me go get him," the woman replied, happily leaving her seat. Abuela looked nervous, and even Tabasco hesitated to commence his usual sniffing.

After a few minutes, Detective Gumble came walking out of his office wearing a lobster-print button-down and a pair of faded cargo shorts. "Hey, Meg—"

"Mari."

"What can I do you for, Mari?" the detective asked.

"My Abuela happened to be on the beach when Maurice May's boat exploded," Mari said, motioning to Josefina. "At first we didn't think there was any connection between her accident that morning and Maurice's murder, but something has happened. I think she might really be in danger."

The receptionist leaned forward inquisitively. "What makes you think that?"

"You know the gazebo in the middle of the farmer's market?" Mari explained. "We were down there buying produce when the roof collapsed. My Abuela had been sitting there just moments before that. And I think there might be a connection between her accident at the beach the day we arrived, and a man the folks around here call Sean Pepper."

Detective Gumble sighed as if annoyed that he was being asked to do actual work. He opened a drawer and pulled out a form. Nodding to Josefina, he said, "Ma'am, could you tell us in your own words what happened?"

"It's just like she said," Josefina replied in Spanish. She often did when she was anxious. Mari translated.

"My Abuela says that she thinks someone might have been trying to harm her, but she happened to walk away from the gazebo in time," Mari said.

"Lucky you," Detective Gumble responded, keeping his gaze on the form.

"Never mind." Josefina gulped, changing her mind.

"Listen." Mari raised her voice. "My Abuela says that she was attacked on the beach by a jalapeño pepper, and then today we saw a jalapeño pepper logo on one of the produce stands. That gazebo cave-in wasn't a coincidence. My Abuela saw something on the day of that boat explosion, and someone is trying to shut her up." Tabasco barked as soon as Mari was finished.

"Attacked by a jalapeño, you say," Detective Gumble replied, chuckling lightly. "Someone must be off of her meds."

Mari slammed her hand down on the desk. Detective Gumble jumped. "My Abuela is not crazy and saying so in front of her is completely unprofessional. Now, I am trying to help you out. You said yourself that your investigation of the explosion was a serious matter. I suggest you talk to this Sean Pepper guy and see where he was at the time ... *detective*."

"Right." Detective Gumble's smile disappeared from his face. He cleared his throat. "I will do that."

As Mari stormed out of the station, she turned to Josefina and said, "I can't believe they treated you like that. I haven't been this upset in a long time."

Josefina shrugged in defeat. "It's no different from how your brothers treat me."

"But that gazebo could have killed you," Mari ranted. "I thought they would be a little more receptive now that you've almost died twice."

As they arrived back at the condo, Mari saw a figure sitting in a car in the parking lot. The windows were rolled down, and Mari saw that it was Shannon May. She was wearing gold-rimmed sunglasses, dark red lipstick, and she was combing her golden hair back into a ponytail.

"Go on inside," Mari said to Josefina. "I'll join you in a few minutes."

Mari took Tabasco to greet Shannon.

"Hi there," she commented. "What are you doing sitting here all by yourself?"

"I'm so sorry for interrupting your holiday," Shannon replied, putting her lipstick back in its case, "but I'm in desperate need of your help. Would you be willing to do me a favor, no questions asked?"

"That depends on the favor," Mari answered with a note of suspicion in her voice.

"Thank you, Mari." Shannon reached into her purse and pulled out a cell phone. "I knew I could trust you. I was going through Maurice's contacts, and I think I may have found a phone number belonging to his mistress. If you could call it for me, that would just be the bee's knees."

"Why do you need me to call it for you?" Mari asked. "Couldn't you just call yourself?"

"I could," Shannon said, "but everyone in town knows my number. I need someone from out of town to call so that whoever is on the other end picks up. Please, I need to know who he was seeing."

"Makes sense, I guess," Mari said slowly. She climbed into the passenger's seat and pulled out her cell phone.

"Just pretend that you're calling a friend," Shannon suggested, showing Mari the phone number.

Mari dialed the number Shannon showed her on Maurice's phone. After two rings a woman's voice answered. "Hello? Who is this?"

Mari realized she would have to think of a name quickly, and she chose the first one that came to mind. "Is Coco there?" she asked.

Mari fully expected the woman to say she had the wrong number, at which point Mari planned on apologizing and asking for the woman's name. So she was surprised when the voice on the other end said in a suspicious tone, "Speaking. Who is this?"

"Is this the Coco who works at the farmer's market?" Mari asked, not able to believe her own luck.

"I'm the only Coco in Pelican Point."

Mari hung up before the conversation could proceed any further. She turned to face Shannon and found that she was crying. Mari bit the side of her lip as she glanced down at Tabasco who had secured a comfy spot in her lap.

"All this time," Shannon said. "I think the worst thing about it is that I was betrayed by my own husband and someone I thought I was my friend. You know, I buy from Coco's stand all the time. How could she? This whole thing just makes me sick."

"Maybe it's not what it looks like," Mari suggested. "I'm sure there's more to the story. Just because Maurice called her a lot that doesn't mean they were lovers."

"There's only one way to find out," Shannon replied, retrieving a compact mirror from her purse and straightening her hair. "I need you to go and talk to Coco for me. I want her to look you in the eyes and tell you she wasn't having an affair with my husband."

CHAPTER NINE

That evening as the sun was setting over Pelican Point, Mari appeared on the front steps of Coco's terraced cottage. She took a deep breath and hoped that she would be able to give Shannon the closure she needed. With the way Shannon had been falling apart over her husband's accident, Mari had felt obligated to help.

Shannon waited in her car behind a row of tall shrubs at the end of the street. On the way over, she had given Mari her instructions to ask Coco about her relationship with Maurice. Mari, who had only undertaken the assignment in the first place out of pity for Shannon, had warned her that confrontation was a bad idea.

Mari wasn't sure she could convince Coco to be a willing participant in her search for the truth. But she'd promised Shannon that she would at least try. Mari knocked on Coco's door uncomfortably and waited.

Coco opened the door with a bowl in her hand. She'd been in the middle of stirring together the ingredients of what looked like a pasta salad. When Coco saw Mari's face, she nearly dropped the bowl in surprise.

"You'll have to forgive me," Coco said, who had her hair up in curlers. "I don't usually get visitors. Hey, you're that girl from the farmer's market. How is your grandmother?"

"Alive," Mari answered.

"Well, that's good news." Coco opened the door wider. "Would you like to come in? I'm very curious as to why you hunted down my address. Can I get you a drink?"

"Just some water, thanks." Mari took a deep and followed her into the living room. She took a seat on a large but not especially comfortable sofa. Coco shuffled out of the kitchen carrying two water glasses, which she placed on the coffee table between her and Mari.

"I know we've met a couple of times at the farmer's market," Coco said as she sat down in a leather recliner, "but for the life of me I can't remember your name."

"It's Mari."

"Mari, right." Coco nodded. "Alright, out with it. You really are my boss, aren't you? You've come here to fire me." She paused and glanced around the room. "Wait, is this one of those TV shows?"

"Coco, there are no cameras." Mari couldn't see any way of avoiding the truth, so she decided to be as candid as possible. "I'm not your boss. I'm here at the request of Shannon May."

The effect of these words on Coco was immediate. Standing up and drawing herself to her full height, she jerked the glass out of Mari's hand and said in a cold voice, "We're done here. You can see yourself to the door."

Mari felt a chill as she watched Coco storm wordlessly into the kitchen, where she began putting away dishes with an unnecessary amount of clatter.

"I don't understand," Mari said, walking in behind her. "What were you doing making all those calls to Maurice?"

"It is private," Coco responded, not even bothering to turn around. "It's none of your business, and if you're not gone within the next minute, I'm calling the police."

"Maurice is dead, and his widow is looking for answers," Mari continued. "Now if you say nothing, Shannon will go on assuming that the two of you were having an affair. She is torn up about it as anyone would expect, but she will move on."

Coco gave Mari a venomous look. "You have no idea what you've stumbled into," she said. "Maurice was a horrible person, and I'm glad he's gone. He was selfish, inconsiderate, ill-tempered, and frankly, his boat business was treading water."

"And yet you still had an affair?" Mari asked, nimbly sidestepping Coco's attempts to distract her from the main issue.

"Yes," Coco said in an exasperated voice. "And I wish I could take it all back. Tell Shannon that I'm sorry, but in the end, Maurice deserved what he got."

Without another word, she escorted Mari to the door.

Mari slowly walked back to the car and started by apologizing to Shannon. "I don't know if it helps," she said, "but I was once engaged to a man who turned out to be ... not what I expected. That's the risk you take, opening up your heart to someone."

"I guess there's some comfort in knowing the truth," Shannon said through tears. "Oh Mari, I'm sorry you had to meet me during one of the worst weeks of my life."

"I'm not offended," Mari replied. "In fact, why don't you have dinner with my family and me tomorrow night?"

Shannon shook her head sadly. "As much as I appreciate your generosity, I wouldn't want to intrude on your vacation any more than I already have. Besides, you'll see me tomorrow night at the annual Pelican Point Seafood Festival. I'll be singing with a local band called The Four Crabs."

Shannon drove Mari back to her condo in the glow of the setting sun. Mari couldn't stop thinking about the conversation she'd just had with Coco. She seldom met anyone with so little remorse for the wrongs they had done. Coco's only regret seemed to be that she hadn't killed Maurice herself.

Maurice's death was looking more and more suspicious, not to mention more and more personal. He couldn't have been killed as part of a sloppy robbery. Maurice had the affections of two women, and both of them were as emotional as ever. There was only one question hanging in the air.

Which woman, if either, was capable of killing?

CHAPTER TEN

Mari entered the condo to find the rest of the family hustling around the apartment. Mrs. Ramirez stood in the living room jangling her keys impatiently while David knocked at the bathroom door. He was wearing a blindingly blue silk shirt and a crisp pair of dress pants.

"Get dressed," Mr. Ramirez said as she walked through the kitchen. "We're going out tonight. I met a guy on the beach who recommended this terrific seafood place."

"And?" Mari narrowed her eyes.

"And the chef knows a guy who can get me half-priced seafood for the restaurant," he confessed.

"Please, tell me you've kept that bit of info from Madre," Mari muttered.

Mr. Ramirez winked at her.

Ten minutes later, the family pulled up outside of a restaurant called *Salt of the Sea*.

"This is the place you were talking about?" Mari asked, a little shocked. "Dad, you've been lied to."

"I realize it's probably not the fanciest place in town," Mr. Ramirez replied, "but it is the cheapest. You won't believe some of the amazing deals they have at happy hour."

As Mari emerged from the car, she gazed skeptically at the tawdry storefront with its grinning lobster sign and the narrow alley filled with trash cans and graffiti. "I'm not sure this is the best idea," she said. "I've heard nothing but terrible things about this place."

"Mari quit being so negative," Alex muttered with a smirk on his face.

"Give it a chance," Mr. Ramirez added. Mari and the rest of the family followed him through the swinging saloon-style doors and into the dim interior.

"Ahoy, there!" came a booming voice as a man wearing a tri-cornered hat and an eyepatch leaped out at them. "Welcome to *Salt of the Sea*. I'm Briny Bill, the manager, and I'll also be your waiter tonight."

"Why, what happened to all your other waiters?" Alex asked.

"Son," Mr. Ramirez scolded him and shook his head.

"Our one waiter," Briny Bill answered, "hasn't shown up to work for the past week if you must know. I've had to work every shift meself. Now, would you prefer indoor or outdoor seating?"

"Outdoor, please," Mr. Ramirez responded.

"Tee-riffic," said Briny Bill, but without much enthusiasm. He led them through the dining area with its low-hanging chandeliers and toward the back patio. From here they had a perfect view of the beach. So far, that seemed to be the only plus.

"See, this isn't so bad," Mr. Ramirez said, rubbing his hands together contentedly. "Sometimes the best places to eat are the undiscovered ones. When I was a boy, your Abuela took Diego and me to a little seafood shack in Galveston. There was a man playing an out-of-tune viola and so many dogs that I was scared to get up and refill my drink. But you know what? That ended up being the best meal I ever had. Remember that, Mama?"

Josefina beamed proudly. "That was the day little Diego decided he wanted to run his own seafood business."

"And the world was never the same," David muttered under his breath.

Mr. Ramirez's enthusiasm lasted exactly as long as it took him to get the menu, at which point he spluttered angrily and rose from the table. "Grab your things," he said. "We're leaving."

"What? Why?" asked David and Alex in unison.

"Because I refuse to pay these prices. Even at half-off, this is outrageous. Look at the price of those onion rings." Mr. Ramirez scowled.

"And it's not even happy hour," Mari commented.

"We might have been here in time if someone hadn't been out sleuthing," David said. Mari rolled her eyes.

Mrs. Ramirez motioned for calm. "Everybody sit down," she said. "We're not going anywhere."

Mr. Ramirez gawked at her as if she had just announced that she was leaving the family to take up piracy on the high seas.

"Do you really expect me to pay these prices, Paula?" he demanded.

"Those prices are perfectly normal," she responded. "They're cheaper than most."

"If it makes you feel any better," Mari added, "I'll pay."

Mr. Ramirez sat down again, looking mollified. "Can you afford that?"

"Probably not on my salary," she said quietly.

Mari not only paid for the whole meal but also ordered drinks and dessert for everyone. By closing time, her mother and father were dancing together under the lights of the patio while her brothers flirted with girls at the bar. Meanwhile, Mari and Josefina enjoyed an enormous tiramisu.

"Maybe Dad was right," Mari said as she fed Tabasco the last bite of tiramisu. "This isn't the greatest place I've ever eaten, but it does have a sort of romantic charm to it."

"It's much better than that awful seafood shack José remembers," Josefina replied. "We had to throw most of our clothes away after we got home. There was so much fur on them. Of course, he doesn't remember all of that. He only remembers the good stuff."

As neither Mari's parents nor her brothers were capable of driving, Mari drove the family home that night. They were still piling drunkenly out of the car together as she approached the front door of the condo.

"This is the key, right?" Mari said, holding up her mother's keychain for her inspection.

"Yeah, yeah, the key—the big key," Mrs. Ramirez answered, breaking heavily.

But when Mari tried to unlock the door, she found that it was already unlocked.

A cold wind swept over the balcony, making her shiver. Josefina clutched her shawl tight. "Y'all stay here," Mari said. "I need to check something."

"Shouldn't we just call the police?" David called after her, but she had already disappeared into the darkness of the condo.

Mari crept through the living room and cautiously turned on the lights. The room looked exactly as it had looked before they'd left. The sandy-colored couch was pressed against the back wall, and cards from her brothers' last game were still untouched on the coffee table. Nothing had been turned over, and nothing appeared to have been stolen. It was the same in every other room in the house.

"Do you smell anything, Tabasco?" Mari asked, but Tabasco merely shook himself in confusion. He didn't know what to make of it any more than she did.

"Weren't you the last one out of the condo?" David asked as the rest of the family filed in. "You probably forgot to lock it."

It might have been a comforting theory if Mari hadn't been certain she had locked it before she'd left. There had been too many strange accidents in the last couple of days for her to be careless. Besides, she always locked her door back home as a precautionary measure. It was a habit.

Her parents and brothers got ready for bed, but Mari remained standing in the kitchen for some time with her senses on high alert. She felt sure someone had broken into the house while they were gone but had left without finding what they were looking for. And the only thing they could have been looking for, the only possibility that made any sense to her, was that they were after Josefina.

CHAPTER ELEVEN

The next day was the first day of the Pelican Point Seafood Festival. Mari woke up early and took Tabasco for a walk on the beach, watching as birds scattered and the fog rolled back at the first light of dawn. Maintenance workers in blue and gray uniforms were already running up and down Pelican Street carrying equipment and setting up booths and displays.

Mari returned to the condo around 8 AM to find most of the family in the kitchen getting ready for breakfast. David had accidentally torn open his package of cereal and was covered in cinnamon sugar, and Alex and Josefina were making breakfast tacos for everyone. Alex fried the eggs and sausage while Josefina grilled her famous handmade tortillas. Mrs. Ramirez hovered behind them, occasionally whispering suggestions until Alex nudged her away.

"Go find something else to do while we finish," Alex said, clutching his forehead in pain. He and David were both suffering the ill effects of last night's drinking. "You're still technically cooking even if you're just telling us how to do it, and that's a violation of Mari's rules."

"Right, the rules," Mrs. Ramirez replied, grabbing her newspaper and heading out onto the back patio.

"Where's Dad?" Mari asked, but before David could answer the front door flew open and Mr. Ramirez bustled in dragging a large blue-and-white cooler behind him.

"You won't believe what I just bought," he said with a boyish grin. "There is so much raw fish packed into this cooler. Pounds and pounds of fish."

Mari, realizing how much money such a purchase would have cost at a reputable place, and knowing that her father would never dare spend that amount, said in a suspicious voice, "Dad, where did you get that?"

"It doesn't matter where I got it," Mr. Ramirez said cheerfully. "The point is that I got it."

None of the Ramirez siblings looked particularly reassured as he opened the chest to reveal a tub full of ice and raw fish. The stench was overpowering, and it sent David fleeing toward the restroom.

"That's gotta be the nastiest thing I've smelled all week," Alex responded, covering his nose. "Are you sure those are safe to eat?"

"Well, there's only one way to find out," Mr. Ramirez replied. "Mari, will you do the honors?"

"You want me to cook the fish?" Mari asked. "For breakfast?"

"Not all of them," he said. "Whatever we don't eat this morning we'll take home. Nobody mention a word of this to our customers, or they'll be knocking at our front door wanting some."

"I don't think you'll have to worry about that," Alex commented.

***

That afternoon the Ramirez family attended the seafood festival which took place on a narrow strip of shoreline near one of the local docks. Men and women in pirate costumes welcomed them onto the crowded shore. There, bikini-clad girls threw cannonballs at plastic ships in the hopes of winning a mermaid t-shirt and a crowd of teen boys watched. The manager of *Salt of the Sea* wandered through the crowd in his three-cornered hat inviting guests to sample his calamari.

"I can't even hear myself think," Mr. Ramirez said loudly. "Why don't we split up for now? We can meet back here later."

"See ya," Alex responded. "David and I are meeting some people anyway."

"Yeah, and I wanted to find more of those amazing fish deals," Mr. Ramirez added. "Paula, come with me." Mrs. Ramirez agreed and took her husband's hand. Mari stayed behind with Tabasco and Abuela.

"Alright," Mari stated, trying not to feel like she had just been ditched by the rest of the family. "What do you want do, Abuela?"

"Find some cool air," Josefina answered, fanning herself. "If I faint now, everyone will think I'm falling apart."

Mari found an empty bench in the shade of a leafy palm tree and left Josefina there with Tabasco while she went off in search of a drink to cool her off. She kept a close eye on her as she waited in line at the smoothie stand, half-afraid that her elusive attacker might suddenly appear.

Mari bought herself an ocean berry smoothie and Josefina a tropical blast and was on her way back to the bench when Tabasco began barking furiously. In the distance, Mari saw a crowd forming around two slender figures. As she came closer, she realized they were Shannon and Coco.

The women stood facing each other as if preparing to duel. Rage was on their faces, scorn in every line of their features. Coco spread her arms out as far as they could go to make herself look bigger than she was. Instead, it looked like she wanted to give Shannon a hug. Shannon, meanwhile, maintained a confident swagger and seemed to be deliberately coaxing Coco's anger in the hopes of being attacked and seeing Coco arrested.

"You look more ridiculous than a one-eyed wombat," said Shannon. "I don't understand wat Maurice saw in you. Who leaves their spouse of twenty years to have an affair with a woman who resembles one of Australia's dumbest marsupials?"

"Someone who was really sick of their marriage," Coco fired back, her curls bobbing. "No one else seems to want to tell you the truth, so I'll tell you. Your hair looks like a nest. Your skin is practically orange from all of the cheap fake tanner, and you smell like my grandma's house.'"

Shannon shut her eyes and counted to three as if trying to restrain herself from launching herself upon Coco.

However, Coco, sensing that victory was imminent, said in a taunting voice, "Your marriage was over a long time ago, and you know it."

"You little hussy!" Shannon shouted, running forward and slapping Coco hard in the face. Mari, realizing a brawl was unavoidable unless someone intervened, dropped her drinks. She grabbed Shannon's arms, but Shannon continued lunging at Coco with all her might.

"Enough," Mari yelled, struggling to pull them apart. "You've both managed to embarrass yourselves in front of the entire town. If you don't walk away now, I'm going to call the police."

"Do it," Shannon said coolly. "I welcome it."

"While you're at it, you can tell them she murdered her husband for the money," Coco responded. "We all know the truth, Shannon. You might as well admit it."

"How dare you," Shannon replied. "You just wait, Coco. Sooner or later, the police will find out what you've been up to." Shannon glanced around at the crowd. "And I'm not a murderer in case y'all were wondering." She turned around abruptly and stormed off.

"I don't know what you're talking about," Coco shouted after her, crossing her arms with a look of disgust. "I have nothing to hide." She turned and walked off in the opposite direction.

Mari left and went back to the spot where she'd left Josefina, feeling relieved that she had prevented Shannon and Coco from killing each other. But her relief turned to panic in an instant when she realized that Josefina wasn't where she'd left her.

"Abuela?" Mari called, but there was no answer. "Abuela?"

Her vision went cloudy, and the chatter of tourists sank to a low and indiscernible murmur as she pulled out her phone. With shaking hands, she dialed Josefina's number. The phone rang twice, three times, and then went to voice mail.

Meanwhile, Tabasco sniffed the area around the bench as if hoping to track her by smell. After a few seconds of doing this, he barked hopefully and took off running. As Mari chased after him, she called her mother.

"I need help," Mari said as she jogged along the beach. "I can't find Abuela anywhere."

"You mean you lost her?" Mrs. Ramirez responded. "I thought you were going to look after her."

"I was, but I had to break up a fight. I'm panicking. I don't know what to do. I'm near the stage where that local band just finished playing."

"We'll be right over," Mrs. Ramirez said, and the hung up.

But the mention of the stage had given Mari an idea. Once at a wedding reception she had seen a young woman take the microphone and announce that her grandpa was missing. If Josefina hadn't been kidnapped, then that was her best chance of finding her.

Mari circled the platform looking for a flight of steps that would lead her up to the mic when Tabasco began barking wildly. Turning around, Mari saw a man wearing a red cap with a tattoo of a jalapeño pepper on his arm. Her eyes met his, and he stood frozen for a second like a raccoon who had just been caught near a trash can.

"Wait!" Mari shouted at him, her suspicions aroused by the look of shock on his face. The man turned and sprinted in the opposite direction.

"Get back here, you evil pepper man!" Mari shouted. But he was already too far ahead. He headed for the docks at a speed she could never hope to match. A second later, he turned off the path and leaped into a large boat. Mari slowed down and breathed a sigh of relief.

There was now no way for him to escape her unless he jumped into the sea.

CHAPTER TWELVE

As Tabasco and Mari neared the boat, there was no sign of the man with the pepper tattoo.

Cautiously, they stepped onto the slippery deck.

"Don't think you can hide from me," Mari called after him. "There's no way off of this boat, and the police are on their way."

This wasn't strictly true. Mari had a feeling that if she called the local police, they would only get in the way. But she thought it might drive the man out of his hiding space.

However, her threats failed to dislodge him. After a few moments of quietly prowling the deck in search of him, Mari heard a muffled banging noise coming from below deck. At the same instant, Tabasco barked and, breaking free of her grip, ran down a narrow flight of steps into the cabin.

There she found a scrawny young man wearing a pair of faded blue jeans and a t-shirt with a picture of an enormous mackerel in a bishop's hat. Sweat poured down his face as he gazed with a bewildered look at a wall full of buttons and levers. Josefina sat on the floor with her back against the wall, her mouth bound with duct tape and her hands tied behind her with bungee cords.

"Where's the man with the jalapeño tattoo?" Mari asked the young man.

"I don't know," the boy wailed, tugging at his badly cut red hair. "I don't know anything!"

"He's a criminal," she said as she knelt down to untie Josefina, "so if you know anything, you should say so."

"I was having a smoke in the alley behind *Salt of the Sea*," he said. "I was approached by a man wearing a red cap. He asked me if I knew how to drive a boat and I said yes."

"Wait, I know who you are," Mari said as she pulled Josefina to her feet. "You're the waiter from *Salt of the Sea*. You've been missing for the last week."

"I lied," he said sadly. "I don't know how to drive a boat. I just wanted to look cool. I figured I could learn as I went."

"Abuela," Mari said, "did this man try to hurt you?"

Josefina shook her head and pointed to the doorway. "It was him!"

A shadowy figure had appeared at the top of the stairs, blocking out the last rays of the setting sun. With his blood-red hat and yellow coat, he was unmistakably the man Mari had chased onto the boat. He wore a menacing look as he slowly descended the stairs into the crowded control room.

"And just what do ye think you're doing?" the man asked in a low and gravelly voice. He was close enough that Mari smelled the odor of garlic and calamari on his breath.

"I know who you are," Mari replied, undaunted by his threatening manner. "You're Sean Pepper."

Sean took off his cap and scratched the back of his head where the hair rose in loose tufts. "What's it to you?"

"What do you want with my Abuela? Why have you been harassing her?"

"She got in the way," Sean said, glaring darkly at Josefina. "I swam to shore just before Maurice May's boat exploded. Nobody noticed except this old woman." He pointed a knobby hand at Josefina. "She watched me come ashore, and when our eyes met, I knew there'd be trouble."

"You deserve to go to jail for what you did," Mari argued. "You killed Shannon's husband."

"I was only following orders," Sean roughly replied. "I was hired to fidget with Maurice's boat."

"You can't evade responsibility that easily," Mari went on, instinctively lodging herself between Sean and Josefina. "Were you the one who destroyed the gazebo in the farmer's market? And broke into our condo last night?"

"Maybe," Sean answered without a trace of remorse. "A good day's work, if you ask me. It's a shame nobody, but you will ever know. Y'all will carry my secret to the bottom of the sea."

"Who hired you?" Mari demanded. But before Sean had the chance to respond, they were interrupted by the noise of more footsteps on the stairs above. A slim figure entered the control room, her curls bobbing in a sprightly fashion with each step she took.

It was Coco James.

CHAPTER THIRTEEN

"Mari?" Coco said as she edged cautiously down the stairs. "What are you doing here?"

"I was just about to ask you the same question," Mari replied, her eyes darting back and forth rapidly from Sean to Coco. "Please don't try to convince me that you just happened to wander away from the seafood festival and into the cabin of this boat."

"No, of course not," Coco said. Turning to Sean, she added, "What did you need me for? When you called, you didn't mention that Mari and her grandmother would be here waiting for me. Is this some kind of intervention? Wait ... is this one of those new reality TV shows? Where's the hidden camera?"

Mari had to think quickly. When Coco's silhouette had first appeared in the doorway, she had briefly wondered if Coco had hired Sean to kill Maurice. But the more she thought about it, the more she realized how little sense that made. Sean had known where Josefina was at all times and had known she was starting to get her memory back. He must have learned her condition and whereabouts from the person who had hired him, and someone who had been in close contact with Mari throughout her trip.

Slowly Sean limped toward the stairs, grabbed Coco, and dragged her into the room. She began to scream, but he placed a rough hand over her mouth. Coco tried to bite him, but his hands were too large, and she couldn't open her mouth wide enough. With a grunt of annoyance, he shoved her toward the back of the cabin where Mari and Josefina were standing.

"Now be quiet," Sean said. "We'll be leaving soon, and you'll be lying at the bottom of the ocean before the owner of this boat realizes it's missing. Captain Ron here knows all about boats." Sean Pepper placed an approving hand on the waiter's shoulder. "He will be taking us for a little ride."

"Yes, because I can drive this thing," Ron said, his voice quaking. "I have been for the past week."

Mari groaned at Ron's transparent deception. The nature of the lie seemed obvious to everyone but Sean. As the two men conferred, Ron scrambled to explain the purpose of the various levers and dials. "This one gets the boat going," he said, touching a red button lightly with one hand. "And this one fires torpedoes at anyone trying to follow us... that is if the torpedoes are still there. I think they might have been moved to the poop deck."

"Sounds made up," Mari couldn't help but say out loud.

"I'll go and check the dock," Sean muttered, temporarily leaving the cabin.

"What's going on?" Coco asked, who was getting more confused by the minute.

As Mari watched Sean disappear into the daylight, she had a sudden feeling that she knew exactly who had orchestrated the murder of Maurice May and the attempted killing of Josefina. Mari shook her head, hoping that it wasn't true.

She chanced a look around the cabin, thinking furiously. She needed to come up with a plan if she hoped to save herself, Coco, and her Abuela from the hands of the true killer.

"I should've known better," Mari said, half to herself. "I am too trusting I guess."

"Bravo, darling, bravo," came a voice from above, and Shannon May descended the stairs beaming proudly. "You figured it all out by yourself. Too bad it wasn't soon enough to save your meddling grandmother. And yourself. *And* Coco. By the way, where's that horrid dog of yours?"

"He must have run off when he smelled you coming," Mari answered snidely. She glanced around, noticing for the first time that Tabasco had not followed her. He was smart not to.

"I hate dogs," Shannon admitted.

"It *was* you!" Coco shouted as if hardly daring to believe she had been right.

She would have flung herself on Shannon if Mari hadn't grabbed her arms. "You killed him. How could you?"

"Don't act like you care," Shannon said, lighting a cigarette and blowing the smoke in Coco's face. "I'm disappointed it took y'all this long to figure it out. And honestly Coco, I had no ill will against you until you started spreading those horrible rumors around town. I mean, I did you a favor. We both know what Maurice was like."

"What are you going to do to us?" Coco asked.

Shannon laughed lightly. Mari marveled at how different she seemed from the grieving widow she had been pretending to be for the past week. "I'm going to do nothing but sit back and watch. The sea and the explosives Sean has placed around the boat will be doing all of the work for me."

Ron gulped and started the boat. As it began pulling away from the dock, Mari said, "But why are you punishing *us*? We didn't do anything wrong."

"You should have minded your own business," Shannon replied with no remorse. "You shouldn't have gone around snooping. You should have left town when you had the chance. Don't blame me for your poor choices, Mari. This is all on you."

"So, you weren't going to kill Abuela?" Mari asked.

"Don't be ridiculous, you stupid girl," Shannon answered. "Once I learned that Sean hadn't done his job properly, I knew that your grandmother had to go. Wrong place, wrong time."

Sean Pepper returned to the cabin with a scowl.

Mari searched their faces, noticing the tension between them. Sean grunted in annoyance but said nothing as he left Ron in charge of the controls and stumped across the cabin toward Mari and her grandmother. Reaching into his pocket, he pulled out a shiny metallic object. Mari's heart leaped into her throat as he pointed it at her.

"Now y'all do as I say," he said, waving the gun in the air, "and I'll have no one arguing or disrespecting me. Shannon, will ya do the honors?"

Shannon came forward clutching a bungee cord with both hands. Coco kept one eye on the gun in Sean's hand and made no objections as Shannon bound her arms and gagged her mouth. Josefina, meanwhile, had taken a rosary from her shirt pocket and was praying silently.

But as Shannon approached Mari, something appeared on the stairs. Tabasco leaped forward out of nowhere and sank his teeth into her skin. Shannon swore loudly and stumbled backward, swatting blindly at the dog.

"Get him off me!" Shannon shouted. "Ouch!"

"Sneaky little pup," Mari muttered with a grin.

"Don't you move," Sean said, aiming the gun at Tabasco and firing a shot. Mari covered her eyes in horror, but Tabasco nimbly dodged his aim as the bullet tore through the floor boards. With great frustration, Sean fired again. And again. His aim was far from the bulldog. Spouts of water shot up through the broken boards, soaking the floor. Tabasco, unconcerned, kept biting Shannon.

"You idiot!" Shannon shouted at Sean. "Do they call you Sean Pepper because your brain is the size of a habanero?"

"I'm just trying to help!" Sean argued, accidentally firing another shot into the floor.

A tremendous noise blasted through the room, and the boat shuddered. Mari guessed that they hit something. She looked for Ron, but he had abandoned his post and was shaking in the corner.

"What do you think you're doing?" Sean shouted at Ron. "Get this boat back on course!"

"I can't," Ron cried, now furiously pressing every button within reach. "All those other times were beginner's luck. I have no clue what to do."

While Sean and Shannon argued over whether or not Ron should be shot, Mari took advantage of the commotion and untied Coco. Grabbing the four life vests that hung on the wall of the cabin, Mari threw one to Coco, one to Ron, and one to her Abuela. Meanwhile, Tabasco, sensing an opportunity, leaped on Sean and began gnawing at his leg.

"Argh!" Sean yelled, stumbling backward as the boat shuddered again. "Get that demon dog off me!"

Once again he took aim at Tabasco, but Mari, who was lighter and faster, grabbed his gun from his hands and fired every remaining bullet into the wood floor.

"What are you doing?" Coco gasped.

"Saving us," Mari replied. "Follow me."

As water streamed into the cabin and Shannon raged at Sean, Mari led Coco and Josefina up the stairs and into the dark water. They were joined a second later by Ron and Tabasco.

"How close are we to shore?" Coco asked.

"Not far," Mari answered. "We should be able to make it back from here."

"We'd better swim fast," Ron said, handing Tabasco to Mari, who licked her face happily. "I heard that lady say she was going to run us down with the boat."

"I'm not too worried," Mari responded, surveying the sinking boat. "I have a feeling she won't get far."

CHAPTER FOURTEEN

"You didn't text me for a whole day," Diego said as his brother came walking through the doors of Lito Bueno's Mexican Restaurant. "I was beginning to think you were dead. You look good, bro."

"Going on vacation has given me a whole new perspective on life," Mr. Ramirez replied, inhaling deeply. "From now on, I'm not going to let the things I can't control get to me."

"You should go on vacation more often," Diego said, looking impressed.

"He should listen to *me* more," Mrs. Ramirez added, rolling her eyes. "If we would have gone on this vacation ten years ago it might have added ten years to his life."

Meanwhile, David and Alex were telling their cousin Cammie tales of Mari and Josefina's heroic exploits.

"I'm starting to think Mari was adopted," Alex commented. "How did our family manage to produce such a savvy sleuth?"

Mari grinned. "Well, it wasn't just me," she said, placing a warm hand on Josefina's shoulder. "I had some assistance."

"And now that you're done being a local hero," Mrs. Ramirez responded, shoving a broom into her hands, "your family needs you. The floor of the hallway is covered in flour for some reason."

"I was testing out a new recipe," Diego said cheerfully. "Unfortunately Cammie didn't notice that the bag was leaking flour until one of our customers pointed it out."

"We agreed not to say anything about that," Cammie whispered.

"Don't worry," Diego replied. "My brother is a changed man. He won't get upset."

Mr. Ramirez closed his eyes and counted to three. "I'm not going to let this get to me," he said quietly. "Everything is fine. The restaurant is in one piece."

As if hoping to test this new philosophy, Tabasco began running rings around the family, barking excitedly.

"That was the most fun I've had in I don't know how long," Mrs. Ramirez continued. "It did cost us a small fortune, and our condo was broken into, and Mari and Josefina nearly died, but I would do it all again if I could. I think we need to do this at least once a year."

"Remember, José," Mr. Ramirez said to himself, "you are in control."

He walked off in the direction of the kitchen while Mari and her mother exchanged glances, looking impressed.

"This vacation really seems to have changed him," Mari said.

Mrs. Ramirez shrugged modestly. "If he's this relaxed now, just imagine how calm he'll be in a couple of summers."

Mari had a sudden vision of her dad clutching a *Salt of the Sea* coffee mug, wearing a flowered lei and Hawaiian button-down, and running through the sand in flip-flops. However, her thoughts were interrupted by a loud noise in the kitchen.

"Diego!" Mr. Ramirez shouted. "What have you done to my kitchen?"

"I love the beach, but it's good to be back," Mari muttered, glancing down at Tabasco.

"I think that's my cue to leave." Diego winked.

BOOKS BY HOLLY PLUM

PATTY CAKES BAKE SHOP COZY MYSTERIES

Until Death Do Us Tart
For Butter Or For Worse
Something Bakes and Something Blue
Frying The Knot
Wedding Bells and a Body
Saying Pie Do

MEXICAN CAFÉ COZY MYSTERIES

Murder Con Carne
Killer Salsa
Smothered In Lies
Rice, Beans, and Revenge

Crimes and Chimichangas
Soft Taco Murder
Murder Con Queso
Jalapeño Killer

Thank you for your support! If you would like to know more about new releases and other fun things, sign up for my author newsletter by visiting my author page on Amazon.com.

Printed in Great Britain
by Amazon